MW01227451

Liar Liar

Is Your Life Based on the Lies You Believe?

SUNDI JO GRAHAM

©2012 by Sundi Jo Graham, Sundijo.com. All rights reserved. First Edition.
©2018 Second Edition.

Cover Design by Donya M. Dunlap

You are welcome to use a short excerpt of this book for review or critique purposes. For more information and other queries, contact info@sundijo.com

All rights reserved.

ISBN: **1718613415**
ISBN-13: 978-1718613416

DEDICATION

This book is for every single son and daughter of God. May you fall in love with who our loving Father says you are and say "No More" to the lies of the enemy. You are loved. You are cherished. You are chosen. **You are redeemed.**

CONTENTS

Liar Liar

Is Your Life Based on the Lies You Believe?

INTRODUCTION

"You is kind. You is smart. You is important."

If you don't already know, that's one of the most memorable lines from the movie "The Help." Whether it was the sweet innocent eyes of a precious blonde little girl or the convincing truth coming from Viola Davis' character, those are words we won't soon forget.

I have to wonder, if we were to fast forward 15 years and ask that little girl if she believed those words, what she would say. If I could guess, her answer would be something like this:

"Why would I believe that I'm kind, smart, and important? I'm lucky to remember my own mother's name since I've spent most of my life in the care of my nanny. I often ask myself if there was something I could have done differently to make her love me. I never do anything right. When she is around she's constantly telling me how I need to do better, look prettier, get better grades, and focus on being perfect for everyone else. I'm just existing, that's all I know to do."

Yes the movie is fiction, but there is more truth behind the story of that little girl than we may realize. Maybe you're that little girl. Maybe you're now a grown woman or man whom desperately wants to believe that you are **somebody.**

I want to tell you the truth today. Allow the words of this book to slap you in the face with a dose of reality. I want to help you stop believing the lies of who you think you are. It is time to take the next step of **knowing** and **believing** who you are.

And you will know the truth, and the truth will set you free." John 8:32, NIV

Do me a favor, if you've decided you're interested enough to keep reading.

Don't just think this is another book by some religious fanatic trying to make you get right with Jesus (AH!)

I assure you of two things:

1. I'm not a big fan of religion myself
2. I'm still trying to get right with Jesus

HI, MY NAME IS

Hi. My name is Sundi Jo. (sun-dee-jo) Let me tell you a little bit about myself. I'm stupid. I'm fat. I'm completely unlovable. My dad hates me and chose alcohol over loving me. I'm too ugly and no man will ever love me. I'll never amount to anything and my mother will never understand me. You're only talking to me because you have an ulterior motive, not because you really want to know anything about me.

Oh.. and how are you today?

If you had met me for the first time nine years ago, those would have been the words swirling around silently in my mind as I shook your hand, smiling and pretending all was well.

I didn't have the first clue how to take a compliment because I didn't believe there was anything good about me.

Something tells me you've been there too.

Allow me to introduce myself now.

Hi. I'm Sundi Jo. I'm beautiful. I'm okay with me. This smile is mine and I love it. Thank you for complimenting my hair – I accept the compliment. My dad loved me through an addiction the best way he knew how. Someday God will provide a man who I will one day call my husband. My mom and I have a healthy relationship and God continues to make it even better. I'm letting my guard down with you because I don't have to be suspicious of everyone.

I'm still a work in progress, but as Joyce Meyer says, "I'm not where I need to be, but thank God I'm not where I used to be."

We let the world tell us who we are. We let others speak lies over us that we start to believe. We let expectations of ourselves and others fill our minds so much that we believe the end will result in failure regardless of what we do.

So untrue.

THE TONGUE

Words kill, words give life; they're either poison or fruit—you choose.

Proverbs 18:21, MSG

I never realized how bad I talked to myself or about myself until others started to point it out to me. The things I spoke about myself was truth, so I thought.

Not only did I talk negatively about myself, my words crushed the hearts of others as well. If I didn't like you, I told you. If you did something to tick me off, I let you know about it in words I can't put in this book. The last thing I cared about was whether or not your feelings were hurt.

Grace was certainly something I had no grasp of, and I'm still a work in progress today of understanding the depths of that powerful word. If I didn't like your idea, "that was stupid!" If I didn't like the way you acted, I wouldn't hesitate to put you down.

I had no idea the destruction I was bringing to the lives of others with my hurtful words. I was oblivious to the wounds I was opening in their hearts because I was too focused on myself. If I could take those things back, oh how I would.

What I'm about to tell you I'm not proud of. I look forward to the opportunity, if God allows, to see this man again and apologize.

Many years ago (waaaayyyyy pre-Jesus), my roommate and friend, who we'll call Nick, who happened to be gay, was having relationship troubles. He often ran to me when things didn't go right, and because I was super co-dependent, the rescuer in me wanted to fix things. So that's what I generally set out to do.

Let's call his friend John. He was confused about his lifestyle choices and it was wreaking havoc on his emotions. He wanted to follow God but he was walking down the wrong path and he knew that. Because of this, he broke off the relationship and my friend was "hurt." I decided to step in. I didn't have a relationship with God at this time and protecting people's feelings was not on my to-do list.

I don't remember the whole conversation, but two things I distinctly remember: I let John know that only losers worked minimum wage jobs at Subway and I called him a faggot. I was determined to put him in his place for hurting my friend.

Yes, I did that. I spoke those words over that man's life. My words were poison to a confused man desperate to do the right thing. The worst part of it? I was living in a homosexual relationship at the time as well. I was living with a woman, confused about my own lifestyle choices, not even pursuing a relationship with God.

What a hypocrite!

Though I have long since been forgiven because of my relationship with Jesus Christ, those words still haunt me today. I no longer live in condemnation because of the words I spoke to John, but it still hurts my heart.

There is now no condemnation for those who are in Christ Jesus. - Romans 8:1, NIV

Even though I have been reconciled in my relationship with God, I long for the day and opportunity to be reconciled with John, a man I barely knew, yet tore apart with the words I spoke to him.

We must protect our tongues. It's a matter of life and death. We have the opportunity to give life to someone with a kind word or bring death to them with condemnation.

STINKIN' THINKIN'

"We need to be very aware of what we choose to think about. Sooner or later the thoughts we build in our minds become words and actions." Dr. Caroline Leaf

The average person has over 30,000 thoughts per day. Isn't that crazy when you think about it? (Pardon the pun) That doesn't include the words we speak, only what we think.

As I was introducing myself previously and sharing my thoughts, that was only in a matter of seconds. So imagine, if you will, the effects that could have on a person if their thinking was negative. It doesn't take long for those 30,000 words to make an impact on our minds, our hearts, and finally, our words.

You are what you think. I'm pretty sure some wise scholar somewhere came up with that long ago.

If you believe you're ugly, does the way you dress reflect your thoughts? Do you cover yourself up? Do you hide? If you change those negative thoughts and begin to think you are beautiful **and** tell yourself the same, watch how your style of dress changes.

Most of my life I wore big t-shirts, long-sleeve shirts, boy shorts, and ball caps: anything to hide the fact that behind the appearance there was actually a beautiful woman in there somewhere. I was too afraid to let people see that part of me. It was too vulnerable and I didn't want to risk being hurt.

Though I still prefer flip-flops and t-shirts to skirts and high heels, I'm comfortable being me.

P.S. When in doubt, add pink to your wardrobe – it changes everything! Yes men, this applies to you as well. Real men wear pink, right?

If you think people will never love you, ask yourself how you do with loving others. Do you tolerate people or do you actually love them? The more you believe that not everyone is out to get you, the more you'll realize how much easier it is to allow others to love you, with no other motive but to simply love you.

Journal Time

Take a few moments and write down the thoughts you've had in the last few days. Were the majority of them negative? Be honest with yourself. No one else has to see the list.

I encourage you to start paying attention to your thoughts. With practice you will become more conscious of what you are thinking about.

LIAR LIAR

You're not good enough. You'll never amount to anything. You have to be perfect. You have to look perfect. You're a failure.

Any of these hitting home with you?

Are there other lies you've believed about yourself, whether they've been words spoken to you, or something you've come up with yourself? Write them down.

As an eight-year old, I specifically remember lies being spoken to me by my third grade teacher. I took them as truth and over the years, those lies were rooted deep within me. I still find myself sometimes having to remember what the truth is.

I have struggled with my weight all my life. Because I was a larger kid, I was an easy target for the wrath of my teacher. She would often make me skip lunch, telling me how fat I was. Not only that, but there were times she would make me run laps around the playground while she shouted obscene words at me. I have to wonder today what was in her heart at that time and pray that God has set her free from the lies she believed.

I believed the lie that I would always be fat. So, what did I do? Ate my feelings away. I protected myself from others by using my weight. I was held in the trap of obesity. I desperately wanted to lose weight and have a life, but I was too scared to allow others to get close to me. The more I believed lies about who I was, the more I turned to cheeseburgers, pizza, and Mountain Dew for comfort.

Until…

I finally stopped believing the lies. I was done letting the words of others and the lies I believed control me. I lost 145 lbs. and replaced that unwanted baggage with truth.

We have to stop letting others control us. We have to take back our minds.

I don't get it perfectly every day. Sometimes I still battle with choosing food as a coping mechanism. Confession: As I write this part of the book, I have an intense migraine because I've been relying too much on sugar to "comfort" me rather than running to the arms of Jesus. But, I've been taking today moment by moment, walking in His grace and refusing condemnation from the liar himself. The devil is a poo poo head.

Earlier I asked you to write down some thoughts. Now take those thoughts and decide which ones are lies.

Next to the lies, write the truth about yourself.

Example:

Lie: *I have to be perfect.*   ***Truth:*** *It's okay to fail.*

WHO AM I?

"Men often become what they believe themselves to be. If I believe I cannot do something, it makes me incapable of doing it. But when I believe I can, then I acquire the ability to do it even if I didn't have it in the beginning." Ghandi

This is the part of the book I've been excited to get to. I want to introduce you to words that can change your life, **if you allow them to.**

Right now you may know yourself solely based on what others have said about you or what you've said about yourself. But the buck stops here.

It's time to believe the truth.

On July 31, 2006 my life was interrupted. I'd heard about this guy named Jesus. People were telling me that he loved me. He died for me. He wanted a relationship with me.

I said my prayers every night since I was a little girl. We're taught that right? *Now I lay me down to sleep… I pray the Lord my soul to keep.* I didn't have a clue what that meant. My assumption was that was my ticket to Heaven. I prayed. I asked God for help when I needed things. I was in.

I was wrong.

Turns out this Jesus is more important than I had realized. **He is the ticket**. If you don't know Him, Heaven ain't happening for you. (That's my sophisticated redneck accent coming out)

I started watching this guy named Ted, a long-haired, Indian worship leader. He was full of grace like I had never seen. He was a man's man, yet he cried when others cried. He loved others in a way I didn't know existed. If that's what following Jesus looked like, I wanted it.

Jesus said in John 14:6, "I am the way, the truth, and the life. No one can come to the Father except through me." Pretty serious stuff, eh?

I tell you this because what I'm getting ready to share with you will do no good if you have no relationship with God. You can't have a relationship with God without accepting that Jesus Christ **died for you.** That's the short version of this amazing story of grace and redemption.

Side note: I'm pretty sure we get all the cheeseburgers, pizza and Mountain Dew in Heaven we want, without the calories of course.

If you are reading this book and haven't yet accepted Jesus, I encourage you to do so now. Pray this simple prayer so that you too can enjoy the benefits of learning **who you really are.**

God, I haven't known you, but I want to. I have made many mistakes in my life, but today I ask for your forgiveness. I accept Jesus Christ as the only one that can save me and today I commit my life to Him. Thank you for loving me and accepting me as your child. In Jesus' name, amen!

And with that ladies and gentleman, I say in the words of Emeril, "Bam, kick it up a notch!"

It's time to learn who you are in Christ. It's time to learn what the Bible says about who you are. These truths will replace the lies you and I have believed too long. I encourage you to speak these truths out loud, as many times as it takes until they sink in.

This practice never stops. It never gets old.

There were times I stood in front of the bathroom mirror and spoke them out loud. Though I felt like an idiot at the time, it did the trick. Actually, I still do it when I feel myself forgetting my identity.

- I am God's child – John 1:12
- I am Christ's friend – John 15:15
- I have been bought with a price and I belong to God – 1 Corinthians 6:19-20
- I have been chosen by God and adopted as His child – Ephesians 1:3-8
- I am free from condemnation – Romans 8:1-2
- I am a citizen of Heaven – Philippians 3:20
- I have not been given a spirit of fear, but of power, love, and a sound mind – 2 Timothy 1:7
- I can do all things through Christ, who strengthens me – Philippians 4:13

This is just a tiny bit of the truth God reveals to us about who we really are. For the complete list, visit sundijo.com/whoiam

Though this won't sink in overnight, I promise, if you repeat these truths out loud, you will start to believe what God really says about you.

Those toxic words, thoughts, and lies you have believed about yourself will eventually disappear and you'll experience a sense of freedom you didn't know existed.

Believe it.

WHAT'S NEXT?

This may be a tiny book, but it's a lot to take in, I know. As I said before, these changes won't happen overnight, but your willingness to change the way you think about yourself will show greater results than you could imagine.

Imagine what we could do with 30,000 positive thoughts everyday?

I'd love to hear what you thought:

- Do you still have questions?
- What do you need help with?
- What did I miss?

I'd love to continue helping you on the journey of learning the truth about who you really are.

Oh… and thanks. You didn't have to read this book, but you did. Thanks for making it to the end and sticking with me.

Do you have a story you'd like to share regarding the lies you once believed? Email it to info@sundijo.com.

#liarliarbook

ABOUT THE AUTHOR

In 2008, Sundi Jo Graham weighed 330 lbs. and was short on hope with no direction of where her life was headed. But after hitting rock bottom, she turned her life around, lost 145 lbs., and committed to helping others find and pursue their passions and God-given dreams.

She is a passionate, versatile, and thought-provoking communicator whose authenticity connects her with audiences in a way few people can.

She is the author of *Dear Dad*, Sundi Jo is a keynote speaker and thought-provoking leader, inspiring women to break free from self-destructive behaviors so they can learn to love themselves and experience lasting transformation through Christ.

She writes at **sundijo.com** on faith and life.

To book Sundi Jo for your next event, visit **SUNDIJO.com/speaking**

Dear Dad, Did You Know I Was a Princess?

Your father. Did he love you enough? Did your relationship with him leave you feeling abandoned, used or unlovable?

Sundi Jo knows this pain. She journaled her way through the childhood wounds that left her with a fortress around her heart and her life on the edge of ruin.

With each entry, you can hear God's pursuit of her. Turn the pages and find yourself nodding in agreement with her questions, her fear, ""Am I beautiful? Am I lovable?"

Don't miss this incredible eyewitness account of God as Father to the fatherless. See His power to overcome what would otherwise destroy a young and innocent heart, even your heart.

Get your copy today at SUNDIJO.com/deardad

Want a More Productive Day?

What if your morning routine is the start of your best day and
your best life?

Sometimes it's hard to get out of bed. The covers are warm. An extra 10
minutes of sleep would be amazing. You put your head under the covers
and beg God for an extra hour in the day, before the day has even started.

The world is waiting for you. Don't sleep your life away. Included in this
FREE eBook are six morning routines you can implement to set you on
course for your **BEST LIFE EVER!**

Get your FREE copy today at SUNDIJO.com/godsbest

74333800R00015

Made in the USA
Middletown, DE
23 May 2018